ISBN: 9798422156962

Foreword

We run a small family MacBook repair shop in Canada, MacBook Medic. We wrote this book to help others learn the craft of logic board repairs.

We'd like to thank our family, friends and the numerous experts who have inspired us along the way. Amongst others: Louis Rossmann, Paul Daniels, Graham (Adamant IT), Piernov, Tim Herrman and Sorin (Electronic Repair School).

Jean & Laurent Debane

MACBOOK LOGIC BOARD REPAIR

HOW TO FIX YOUR MACKBOOK

Jean & Laurent Debane

INTRODUCTION   1

LOGIC BOARD TROUBLESHOOTING FOUNDATION   5

  TROUBLESHOOTING IN CIRCUIT   8

  READING SCHEMATICS   11

  HOW MACBOOKS WORK   13

  POWER ARCHITECTURE   14

  TOOLS OF THE TRADE   16

  SCHEMATICS & BOARDVIEW   20

  TIPS & TRICKS   22

  DO & DON'T   26

TROUBLESHOOTING FUNDAMENTALS   28

  TROUBLESHOOTING SEQUENCE   29

  DEALING WITH CORROSION   33

  SHORTS TO GROUND   34

  VOLTAGE INJECTION   36

  PPBUS FULL VS PARTIAL SHORT   37

  RESISTANCE AND DIODE MEASUREMENTS   39

    SPECIAL CASE 1: CURRENT SENSING RESISTORS   40

    SPECIAL CASE 2: DROP DOWN RESISTORS   41

  COMPONENT TESTING   43

    TESTING MOSFETS   43

    PASSIVE COMPONENTS   44

  MACBOOK DISSASEMBLY   46

MACBOOK REPAIR FUNDAMENTALS   47

  WORKING WITH HEAT   47

  WORKING WITH THE SOLDERING IRON   48

  WORKING WITH HOT AIR   49

BGA CHIPS   52

TO WICK OR NOT TO WICK   53

REBALL WITH SOLDER PASTE   54

WORKING WITHOUT STENCILS   55

BGA REHEAT VS REFLOW   55

REPAIRING DAMAGED TRACES AND PADS   56

REPLACING CONNECTORS   57

ULTRASONIC LOGIC BOARD CLEANING   59

QUICK REFERENCE CHARTS   61

SECTION ONE: KEY POWER RAILS   62

SECTION TWO: OTHER VOLTAGE RAILS & SIGNAL LINES   63

SECTION THREE: KEY ICs   65

SECTION FOUR: TESTING FOR DEAD MOSFET & IC CHECKLIST 66

SECTION FIVE CD3215   67

BASIC POWER SEQUENCE   68

TROUBLESHOOTING CD3215   70

OTHER PROBLEMS   71

INTRODUCTION

We developed this guide to document our journey learning MacBook logic board repairs. If you are new to the field or still learning the ins and outs of board repair this guide will provide you with hundreds of pointers to improve your skills. The book explains the most common faults preventing the MacBook from turning on and how to fix them. Unsure how the key chips turn on? How to test for shorts without frying your board? How to test Mosfets? How to reball chips? This book is for you! Learning these skills will get you on your way to address power issues in any MacBook as well as other laptops as they all work in a similar way. While there are 100s of videos on the subject, there is no real documentation to help someone new to the field tackle these repairs and avoid the common mistakes we all make in the beginning. This is the void this guide is addressing. I can't guarantee that what worked for us will work for you but we are confident that you will find in this guide useful and practical information usually gathered over years of practice.

WHAT THIS GUIDE IS ABOUT

The objective of this guide is to provide practical pointers to troubleshoot and repair the most common MacBook power issues. This is not a book about electronic circuits theory and we try to steer away from technical jargon. Rather the emphasis is on explaining in simple terms the essential information you need to troubleshoot common faults.

One of the advantages of learning to repair MacBook boards vs other laptops is that Apple tends to keep the same chip naming convention and similar designs from model to model. If you learn how to repair a MacBook you can pretty much repair them all. There are changes from year to year such as the shift from MagSafe to USB-C charging ports and more recently the M1/M2 models, but generally once you develop an understanding of the basic MacBook architecture, you can transfer your knowledge to troubleshoot other models easily.

This book uses examples based on specific models and your situation may be a little different. If a required signal is sent from the ISL to the SMC maybe on your board this signal name is a little different or the SMC number is different but the principle should apply; you must adapt these principles and concepts to your situation. What's important is that you develop a basic understanding of how things work and apply that knowledge to your specific situation. Don't try to memorize every chip number, rather try to develop a high level understanding of what each chip does, what are their triggers and where the output goes.

To complement this guide, I invite you to visit some of the excellent YouTube channels on MacBook repair. Amongst others: Louis Rossmann, Paul Daniels, TCRS Circuit, Adamant IT, NorthridgeFix and Electronic Repair School.

MOST IMPORTANT ADVICE

Did you fall when learning to ride a bike? Of course. Eventually you got it and falling is no longer something you need to worry about. This applies to every new learning with many moving parts. If you are new to board repair, <u>never attempt a repair you haven't done successfully on a practice board.</u> Repairing boards is not hard but there are many "gotchas", mistakes we all make in the beginning. For example, replacing a typical BGA chips is not hard but if you have never done it, many things can go wrong: pulling pads, bridging pads, killing chips by applying incorrect heat, flying the chip of the board, knocking off components, etc. Making mistakes is part of learning board repair. The only question is do you want to make these mistakes on the board that is important to you or on a practice board? The good news is we rarely make the same mistake twice. So attempt the different kinds of repair on a practice board and when you master them, do them on a real board. From then on, you should be good to go and overtime repairing boards will become as easy as riding your bike.

Disclaimer: there is always a risk of breaking something while attempting a repair – always do your research, put safety first, when in doubt consult a professional and remember to perform new repairs on practice boards first!

TROUBLESHOOTING MINDSET

Logic board diagnostic requires applied logic and reasoning. Your board isn't possessed; there is always a logical reason why something does not work. The worst approach is to pull components left and right hoping the problem magically solves itself. There are hundreds of components on the board; are you going to start pulling them out until the board comes back to life? Of course not. Based on the evidence, you need to make sound hypotheses about what is most likely causing the board not to turn on and focus on that area. Most times you can test your hypotheses without pulling any component but if you need to pull any, remove only one component at a time. If the component wasn't at fault, put it back right away before you end up with several desoldered components and losing track of where they go. Also, keep wearing your "thinking hat" at all time. Some people would replace a blown fuse and call it a day. Generally a blown fuse is a symptom of another problem. Replacing a fuse without investigating if something else has caused it to blow is not a proper fix. It could blow again or even worse not blow and fail to protect other components from frying. Never pull out/ replace a component or inject power without a sound rationale to do so and always take the safety precaution discussed in this book before injecting power. Finally, always think twice before doing anything that may make things worse such as frying the CPU. Let's fix boards, not kill boards!

All this being said, if you have the right mindset and make the effort to learn the core fundamentals, you will find that fixing logic board is highly doable and satisfying.

IDENTIFYING POTENTIAL PROBLEM AREAS

When undertaking a diagnostic, it's important to develop the ability to zoom quickly on the most likely problem area.

The first principle is to search for clues **at the earliest point** of potential failure. The reason for this is simple. Many problems originating "early in the chain" will cause failure symptoms later in the chain. For example if PPBUS voltage is missing, the other rails created from PPBUS will not be there. There is no point in troubleshooting one of these downstream rails before ensuring the problem does not originate on PPBUS. That's a general rule; sometime a problem down the line will create a problem upstream such as a blown downstream Mosfet.

LOGIC BOARD TROUBLESHOOTING FOUNDATION

You don't need to be an expert in electronic repairs to troubleshoot logic boards, you simply need to develop a basic understanding of how things work to be able to test if what is supposed to be happening is happening, and if it's not, how to identify the root cause of the problem.

Try to develop the ability to look at a schematic and develop a general idea of the inputs and outputs of the chips. Also practice finding quickly where power rails and signal lines get created. If you can become relatively good at these two things, you are well on your way to be able to troubleshoot the most common problems.

On a logic board there are a bunch of ICs and gates that are driving everything. They have voltage inputs and sensor inputs and in turn deliver voltage outputs and sometimes signal outputs to other chips. When we troubleshoot logic boards, we are essentially assessing if the inputs and outputs of each chip are happening and if not, why not. Troubleshooting requires a basic understanding of how these things are supposed to work and a good dose of common sense.

In most cases troubleshooting is not overly complicated. Your amp meter may have already provided hints before you even looked at the board. If the AMP meter is not reading 20V, the problem is on the PP3V42 rail. If the meter reads low amperage, it's likely a PPBUS issue. Very often you won't even need your amp meter as the board is providing you visible clues of what's wrong: water damaged area or components in bad shape – discolored (even so slightly) or blown. People new to the field often inspect the board too quickly and miss these clues. When in doubt slow down, it can save you many hours of unnecessary troubleshooting down the line.

If there are no visual clues... then it's time to get your multimeter, schematic and boardview ready and test your power rails. Let's assume one is shorted. You inject voltage, identify the faulty component and replace it. These three examples are more common than you think and don't require very deep expertise to carry through.

In the majority of cases, "no power" problems will pertain to something on the PP3V42 or PPBUS rails. It's important to take the time to understand the sequence of events for these two rails as you will deal with them often. If these two rails are good we move on to test the voltage on other rails which we can identify with the power rail aliases page in the schematic. If a rail is missing, we investigate: is it shorted? Is the Mosfet good? Is the power regulator getting what it needs to activate this rail?

Troubleshooting beyond this point (not a short problem and no obvious visual clue) requires a basic understanding of how the board works, especially the ICs. Troubleshooting logic boards at the chip level (IC) is a big part of logic board repair. Now let's dive a little deeper on each element.

INPUT VOLTAGE If a chip is not getting it's input voltage, maybe the voltage line is shorted, the line is broken, the voltage is not right, another chip involved in supplying the voltage does not have the conditions to let the voltage flow or that supply chip is broken. That's essentially what we do when troubleshooting voltage input issues. <u>We start from what should be happening and then look into what are the different elements on that chain that may prevent this from happening.</u>

INPUT SIGNALS If a chip receives its input voltage and does not deliver its output, we check if there are conditions that should be met before that chip releases its output. These conditions could pertain to sensing circuit, feedback loops, clock signals, drop voltage lines, "thumbs up" signals from other chips, these kinds of things. Many things could mess up the expected input to the chip preventing it from delivering its output: faulty resistors (big one), capacitors shorted to ground, a chip involved in the supply that did not get what it needs to release the signal, a cold solder joint or a corroded trace preventing a required signal from being delivered.

OUTPUTS If a chip is getting what it needs: input voltage, input signals, and feedback loop (optional) and it's still not releasing what we expect from it, then it is probably bad and needs replacing. But wait, maybe the chip is good but water damage messed up some contacts underneath the chip. Hey let's reheat (kill shorting junk) or reflow (resolder cold joints) and fix potential contact problems and test again. That's the kind of mindset required to fix logic boards.

If each IC chip gets its input voltage, its input signals and delivers it's expected outputs then you most likely have a working logic board and the ultimate reward, a fan spin!

You see troubleshooting logic boards involves having a basic understanding of what should be happening and being able to investigate the different reasons that can prevent what should be happening from happening. That's essentially it. Unless you face a very tricky problem, there is no need to understand the nitty gritty of what every signal and power line do.

As a side note, water damage situations are probably the most frequent driver for logic board repairs. When a board is water damaged, it is very likely that at least one of these two things happened and needs fixing: corrosion breaking signal paths and preventing voltage from flowing or corrosion debris creating problematic bridges (shorts) under chips.

TROUBLESHOOTING IN CIRCUIT

Voltage is the only test you will perform with power ON (unless you own an oscilloscope). All the other tests require your board to be disconnected from power (charger and battery). Some troubleshooting can only be done in circuit such as checking voltage, locating shorted rails or broken lines between components. You can also do many useful component level testing in circuit, but not all. For example, you can't test capacitance in circuit without sophisticated equipment but you may be able to test if a specific capacitor is internally shorted (became a wire) as long as it is not connected in parallel with other capacitors. If a short exists on a rail, all capacitors connected in parallel will appear shorted.

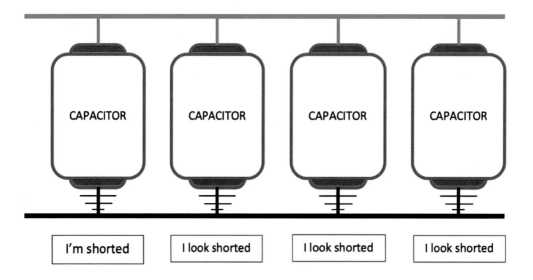

When measuring resistance between two points, <u>you are measuring the path of least resistance between these two points and that path may not be the component you think you are measuring!</u>

If the path of least resistance happens to be the component you are measuring then great, but if the line has lower resistance, you are in fact measuring the resistance of the line. Let's say you are measuring a 10K resistor on a healthy rail with 800K ohm resistance. In this case, the path of least resistance is the resistor and that's what you would most likely be measuring. Now if that line has a partial short of let say 50 ohms, whatever component you may be measuring on that line would likely give you a reading close to 50 ohms unless you are measuring something with lower expected resistance such as a fuse.

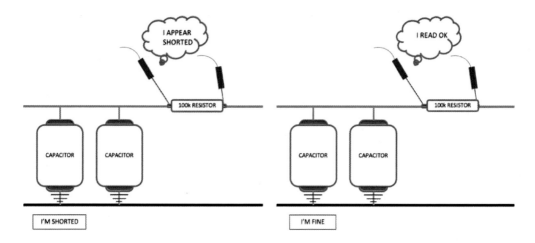

Another situation to be aware of especially when testing if components are internally shorted is <u>what else may also be connected in parallel with the two points you are measuring.</u> For example it is very common to have a loop connecting the Mosfet gate and source with a resistor on that line.

If you put your probes on Gate and Source trying to measure the internal Mosfet resistance, what you would be measuring is the resistance of the resistor unless the Mosfet has lower resistance. Let's say the Gate to Source reading is 200K ohms and the resistor is also 200K ohms, then you can conclude that both the resistor and the gate are not shorted. Let's say instead of 200K you read 50 ohms between Gate and Source. Then something is not right, it can be the resistor or the Mosfet that is shorted. You have to remove one of these components to test it. It seems complex but it's simply common sense as long as you remember <u>that what you are measuring is the lowest resistance path between two points.</u>

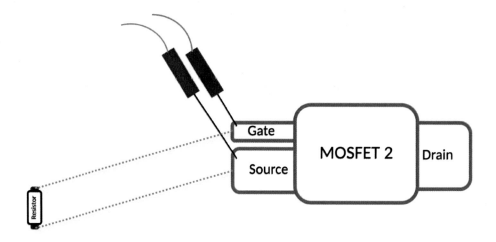

PASSIVE COMPONENTS TESTING

All passive components such as resistors, fuses, diodes, inductors and filters can be tested with resistance, even capacitors. As long as the rail is not shorted (or low ohms), testing these components by placing your probes on their opposing contacts can usually provide some cues of what is not working right. As mentioned previously, always disconnect power before testing resistance. Generally, capacitors fail by becoming shorted. The opposite applies to filters and coils (rare); they become open and do not let voltage through. Resistors tend to fail both ways (too much or too little resistance). Diodes fail by becoming open or shorted in both directions. See troubleshooting section for detailed troubleshooting procedures. Finally, when troubleshooting missing PPBUS downstream rail don't forget to check <u>if voltage is present on both sides of the PPBUS fuse</u>.

READING SCHEMATICS

- Learn to recognize the basic component symbols and acronyms. The first letter is the component type.
C=Capacitor L= Coil F=Fuse Q=Mosfet R=Resistor,
U= Integrated Circuit (in this example a logic gate).

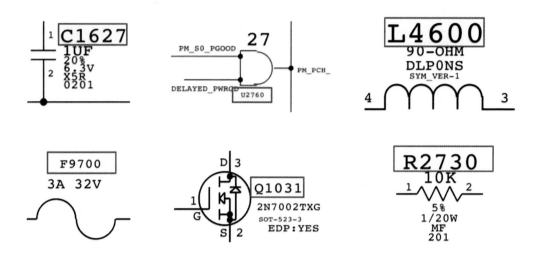

- For IC, generally enable input signals are on the left, voltage input on top and chip outputs on the right but it's not always the case. Pay attention to the function hint of each signal.
For example VIN = VOLTAGE IN, EN or ENTRIP = ENABLE IN.

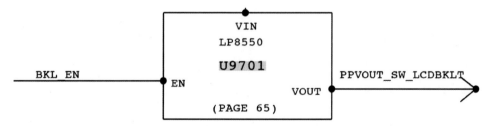

- There are two types of voltage lines on schematics. Power lines identified with a PP prefix and signal lines identified with a single P prefix.

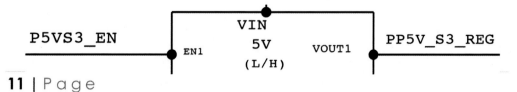

- Schematics provide each component on the board with a unique ID as well as its specifications which is essential when trying to determine if a component is faulty or when you need to find a replacement part.

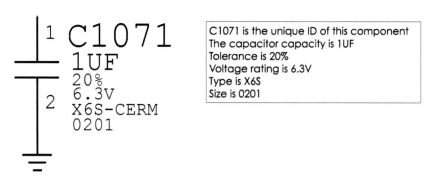

- Schematics are a series of "from to" maps. It takes practice to understand how things flow. When troubleshooting a circuit you usually try to identify where a given line is created. Here's an example clearly showing where PPBUS gets created. The ISL chip input is DCIN and its output is PPBUS (after its transient name PPVBAT).

- Beware that the line name can change as it travels from one component to the next - see Power Rail Aliases page in the schematic for all the name variations.

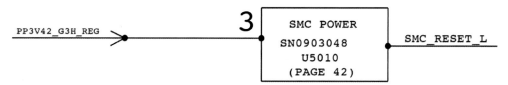

- Schematics document the voltage that should be present on each rail. For example, PP5V_S0 stands for 5V present when the board reach S0 state. PP3V42_G3H stands for 3.42V and G3H means always on.

HOW MACBOOKS WORK

The board powers in sequence from S5 to S0 rails. <u>All rails</u> from the previous state must generally be present before the next state comes on: S5 rails before S4 rails and so on. When all rails for a state are present an enable signal is released to initiate the next rail power on sequence.

G3H rails are the always on rails (before S5 state). They are PP3V42_G3H (PP3V3_G3H on USB-C units) and PPBUS_G3H which powers all the other rails. Please note that whenever we mention PP3V42 in this document it applies to PP3V3 USB-C MacBooks as well.

There are many other power rails in a MacBook. All of them work in a similar fashion and they each have their own power supply & coil. When you see a coil, that's a power rail (except for the CPU/GPU that can have more than one coil on a rail). Each rail circuit is typically composed of:

a. Mosfets which act as switches to let voltage go to the rail and can also work in tandem to create a specific voltage by turning on and off in sequence. Mosfets have 8 pins but only 3 terminals: Gate, Source and Drain. The gate acts as a switch and lets the voltage flow between source and drain.

b. A coil to smooth out voltage & resist rapid voltage changes.

c. A bunch of resistors to deal with spikes or alter voltage/current (eg drop down, current sensing).

d. A bunch of capacitors doing different things whether they are placed before or after a coil. A group of capacitors placed before a coil are acting as reserved power for the coil. When placed after the coil, their role is to smooth out voltage and remove unwanted frequencies (decoupling).

e. Diodes - to allow voltage to flow one way.

POWER ARCHITECTURE

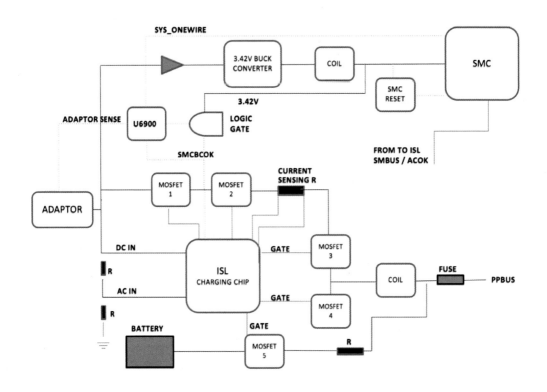

CREATION OF PP3V42_G3H

A buck converter (eg U6990) converts charging or battery power to 3.42V. This is the first rail that turns on. This 3.42V rail powers the SMC. The ISL charging chip also receives a feed from 3.42 but its main power comes from DCIN/ACIN.

For the SMC to turn on it needs the 3.42V input and also a reset signal from the SMC reset chip. When all this happens, the ISL will release SMC_BC_OK allowing the logic gate (U6901) to inform U6900 that it is ok to let the SMC "sysonewire" talk to the charger "adapter sense" and request 20V.

If the above works, we typically have 20V at the charger and a green light on MagSafe models.

CREATION OF PPBUS_G3H

At this point, the SMC will instruct the ISL charger chip to create PPBUS @ 8.6V/12.6V on Air/Pro. Remember that you can't get PPBUS without the ISL and the SMC being powered on and talking to one another. If PPBUS voltage is slightly below what it should be eg 12.4v vs 12.6 volts, then the SMC has not turned on.

These two power rails are a little different than the other rails as they deal with different power sources and voltages (battery and charger) and voltage flows in different ways (from charger to battery and power rails and from the battery to the rails). Most MacBook power problems pertain to these two rails.

When these two rails have proper voltage, the basic power base is operational and it is an important milestone. PPBUS is ready to supply all the other rails in the system.

The other rails rely on power regulators such as buck converters (step down voltage) or boost circuits to modify the voltage received by PPBUS to create the voltage required on that rail. These rails power in sequence based on the state they are associated with: S5, S4, S3, up to "power on" state S0. Typically the SMC, PMIC and PCH work in tandem to confirm the requirements for a given state have been achieved in order to release the signal to turn it on. Please consult the reference chart at the end of this guide for more information on these trigger signals.

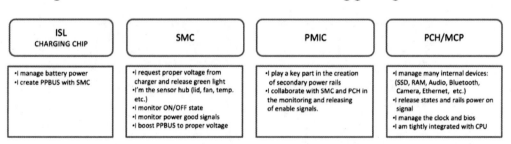

ISL CHARGING CHIP	SMC	PMIC	PCH/MCP
•I manage battery power •I create PPBUS with SMC	•I request proper voltage from charger and release green light •I'm the sensor hub (lid, fan, temp. etc.) •I monitor ON/OFF state •I monitor power good signals •I boost PPBUS to proper voltage	•I play a key part in the creation of secondary power rails •I collaborate with SMC and PCH in the monitoring and releasing of enable signals.	•I manage many internal devices: (SSD, RAM, Audio, Bluetooth, Camera, Ethernet, etc.) •I release states and rails power on signal •I manage the clock and bios •I am tightly integrated with CPU

TOOLS OF THE TRADE

If you're just starting out, here are the minimum essential tools you will need apart from a basic auto-ranging multimeter and a fume extractor.

SOLDERING STATION

A basic station such as an 852D model includes a basic iron and hot air station and can get you started. If you want to go next level up, consider the Atten St-862 or a Quick 861DW hot air station. The Aixun T3A is also a very good value and performs as well as units costing many times more.

KNOCKOFF 852D	AIXUN T3A	ATTEN ST-862	QUICK 861DW

MICROSCOPE

Expect to pay at least $300 for a basic Amscope such as model SW-3T24Z. Basic models lack a zoom function and the field of view is very narrow, a few centimeters at best.

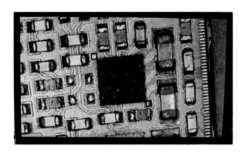

Fixed zoom microscope

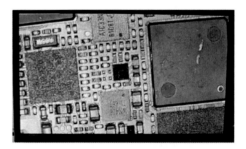

Microscope with zoom-out capability

While a fixed zoom microscope works perfectly for repairs, for board inspection it is highly desirable to have the ability to zoom out to inspect a larger area of the board. Going a step up, a better setup for PCB work includes a microscope with zoom function, 7to45 magnification paired with 10X eye point. These can be purchased in different form factors; fixed base, articulated arms etc. If you have the required desk "footprint", a very good value is the double boom Parco Scientific PA-5F at less than $400.

Always a good idea to buy a microscope with simul focal in case you ever want to add a camera to your setup. Regarding cameras, most of them in the $200+ range paired with an adjustable ring light work quite well. The currently best in class but pricey are models based on the Sony IMX-290 autofocus sensor. Autofocus is not essential as once the camera is set properly it will stay in focus with the microscope. If you find your microscope sits too close to your working surface you can add a .5 Barlow lens allowing you to double the microscope height while maintaining the field of view. Finally, if you really want to go on the cheap, you can buy a basic PCB digital microscope for around $100.

| ARMSCOPE SW3T24Z | PARCO SCIENTIFIC PA-5F |

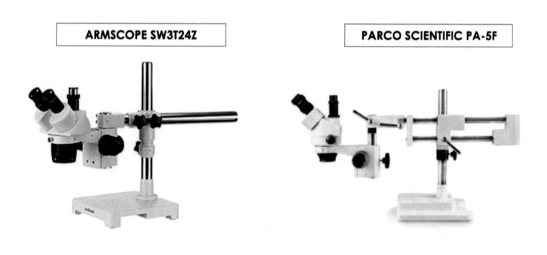

POWER SUPPLY

A basic 5A switching power supply is all you need to get started. You can get one for less than $150. The non-programmable ones all work pretty much the same way. With nothing connected, set amp to the max, then adjust for the voltage you want eg 1 volt. Turn the power off, connect the leads to your board and put the power back on. If you also want to set AMP limit, after you set the voltage you would short the leads, adjust the amp limit, turn the power supply off again and then connect the leads to your board. The voltage that has been set will be maintained unless the amp limit is reached, in which case the voltage will be reduced to ensure you don't exceed the amp limit. Setting amp limit is usually not necessary when testing for short as what matters is controlling carefully the voltage going to the board.

USB AMP METER

Ideally get one with both USB-A and USB-C. Amp meters are cheap and essential for troubleshooting. For MacBooks with MagSafe connectors the bench power supply acts as an amp meter. You need to sacrifice a MagSafe 1 or 2 cable (or buy only a replacement cable) in order to connect it to your power supply and monitor the amp your board in taking for a given voltage.

KJ-KAYJI AMP METER	SKY TOPPOWER STP3010

THERMAL CAMERA

A thermal camera is not essential as there are other ways to identify a shorted "hot" component; you can use your fingers, Isopropyl, upside-down dust can or freeze spray to get the job done. This being said a thermal camera speeds up the process and can sometime identify a tricky component that other methods can't. Stay away from the cheapest models. Below $500, I can recommend these two models: the Seek Compact PRO and Infiray C200/C210. Note that will need a micro lens ($30-$50) specific to these models to do close-up pcb inspections.

SeeK Compact PRO

CompactPRO

Infiray C210

BASIC SUPPLIES

At the very minimum, get yourself some good quality 67/33 solder (.15 or .3MM), flux, wick, 90%+ isopropyl, a good set of electronic repair screwdrivers, very fine tweezers (straight and curved), a silicone mat, shielded jumping wire and solder mask/light and you can tackle most basic repairs. In the beginning, solder paste, solder balls and stencils are optional. You may not face an IC chip replacement in some time and if you do, you can always buy the chips "ready to install" on eBay or AliExpress which will not require reballing unless you messed it up and need to reinstall it.

SCHEMATICS & BOARDVIEW

To get started you need a pdf reader and a boardview software. I recommend the free openboardview to start. Google your logic board model number to find schematics and boardview files. You should be able to find them.

Schematics and Boardview work together. Each component has a unique number so you can easily find a specific component in both tools. Schematics provide component specifications and rail maps. Boardview help you locate where these components are on the board. Boardview is also helpful to trace signals. Let say you're inspecting PP3V42. Click on a pad of a component connected to PP3V42 and all the components connected to PP3V42 will light up! Very helpful when checking whether traces are still working after liquid damage.

Boardview is also useful to confirm BGA chip orientation, which the schematic can't do (locate pin 1 relative to the board orientation and align with the dot on the chip).

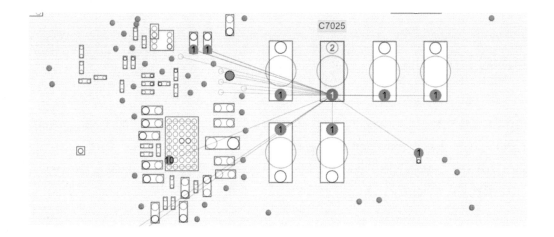

When troubleshooting, we constantly go back and forth between the two tools; they are really indispensable. If you start doing repairs on a regular basis consider the excellent boardview software Flex BV from Paul Daniels allowing you to see a component in the other tool without having to search for it again.

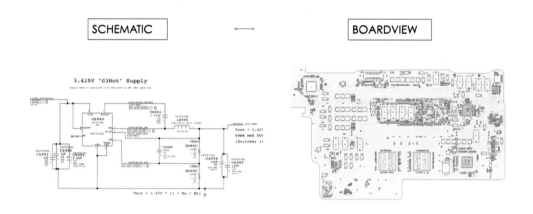

ASD DIAGNOSTIC

Apple has created ASD diagnostic programs for each model. They may help troubleshoot problems, especially sensor type problems. Again, google is your friend to find the specific diagnostic program for your model.

REMINDERS AND TIPS & TRICKS

AMP METER DIAGNOSTIC

If you don't get 20V check PP3V42. If you don't get close to 1 amp, check PPBUS first.

SUPPLYING POWER TO LOGIC BOARD

You can only plug a charger when all ICs are on the board but you can inject voltage on a rail with missing chips to diagnose a short. The only exception to this rule is PPBUS: make sure all downstream Mosfets are good before injecting voltage to PPBUS.

Never power a board when it's still hot after a repair, let it cool down first.

LET BOARD COOL TO GET ACCURATE READINGS

Resistance will be lower when the components are hot. Wait till the board cools down before measuring anything.

YOUR BOARD IS TALKING TO YOU

Normal fan spin:	You are in S0 state and the computer turns on!
Fan on high:	Typically a failed sensor
One Chime:	CPU is ON. Useful to diagnose no image vs no CPU.
No Chime:	Cannot verify RAMs
Three chimes:	Bad Rams

SMC BYPASS MODE

Bypass mode disables SMC sensors. This can be useful to confirm if a nonworking board works when the SMC sensors are off. Disconnect all power, press power button, connect MagSafe and keep power button held for 5 to 10 seconds. Fans should go at max speed.

CLEANING FLUX

Windex sometimes works better than Isopropyl (IPA) to remove stubborn flux residues. Qtips or a brush such as a toothbrush are typically used to remove flux residues. It's good practice to wipe away or blow off residues while it's wet, otherwise you get some dissolved flux reforming on the board as it dries.

BOARD WATER DAMAGE

First clean up the area with IPA (Isopropyl) and a soft brush. If corrosion remains, apply flux and gently scrape away any visible corrosion with a "throw away" iron tip. Finally reheat or reflow the area if it is safe to do so. If there are nearby chips with underfill do not reheat or reflow the area. You should rethin pins/pads after you removed corrosion from these contacts. Finally, verify that any signal touching a pad affected by corrosion is still working after cleanup by testing for conductivity between these pads and where they go. If some pads are dead and no longer carry signals, you will have to install wire jumpers and/or replacement pads.

ISOLATE SOURCE OF THE PROBLEM

If your troubleshooting is not helping you identify the source of the problem, it may be helpful to remove a coil or a fuse on a rail to identify if the problem comes from the source side or the load side.

For example, you can remove the PPBUS fuse(s) to see if the problem is with the creation of PPBUS (ISL side) or downstream by comparing the resistance to ground of these two pads. This approach can also help troubleshoot low PPBUS voltage by checking if PPBUS is back to normal when the other rails are disconnected.

Logic board works outside but not in the case

If the logic board works (fan spin) when taken out of the laptop but stops working when back in the laptop then the issue is with an external component (screen, touch pad, keyboard). A shorted connector can also shut down the computer.

Random crashes

Often due to failing CPU Mosfets, especially on 2013-15 boards.

Board attempts to start then stop (high amp then low)

No short, all rails powered up. Can be a clock problem, check your clock chip.

Recovery mode

Newer MacBook stuck in recovery: the only thing you can do is **DFU revive** with another Mac and hope for the best. If unsuccessful, likely a **T2 Nand** issue - not good.

SHOPPING FOR CHIPS

- Genuine new chips (not reballed) will have lead-free solder (require more heat).
- Chip numbers tend to reflect board numbers. As each MacBook model has many different board numbers, the same MacBook will have different numbers for the same chip. Some chips numbers don't matter but sometimes they do. As an example, you can't replace an SMC from a 2016 1708 on the same 2017 model.
- Some chips are available new but many times you only have used options. Chips involved in managing charging and negotiating power with charging port are subject to abuse and should be bought new whenever possible.

ANTENNA CABLES

Always pry antenna cables from **the back** (cable side), not the front.

RUBBERY COMPOUNDS

If there is a rubbery compound "overlay" on the chip or nearby a repair remove it before applying high heat to the area. 100C is usually sufficient to soften it and facilitate scraping it off.

BOARD 820-2355

Most boards power on when connected to an external power source. A known exception is 820-2355. You have to explicitly turn on this board to get a **fan spin.** To manually turn on any board you have to momentarily short the SMC power ON/OFF signal, often called SMC_ONOFF_L, with ground.

DO

- **DO** disconnect all connectors starting with the battery before troubleshooting a logic board. With USB-C MacBooks, you need to disconnect the flex battery data cable first. Then remove the battery power screw and carefully lift the tab a little.
- **DO** remove removable hard drives - heat will destroy them.
- **DO** use flux when removing components, especially if you're not sure if the component is usable again. The only exception to this is when you really want to reduce heat exposure to adjacent components.
- **DO** use heath shields (top) and heat sink (bottom) to protect the board before using hot air. You can even place an old hard drive under the board to act as a heatsink.
- **DO** a detailed and thorough visual inspection. A missed clue could result in several hours of unsuccessful diagnostics. The visual inspection covers:
  a. Obvious source of component stress (discoloration, bulging, cracking)
  b. Signs of corrosion
  c. Signs of distressed traces
- **DO** pay attention to chip orientation – there is usually a dot representing pin 1. Use boardview for proper orientation.
- **DO** pay attention to directional components such as diodes. While most capacitors are non-directional, some are.
- **DO** be careful when scraping off corrosion. There is likely ground underneath or nearby the pad you are scrapping off. Again, we want to fix problems, not create bigger ones.
- **DO** hold your component with your tweezers from the top so the bottom can make good contact with the board before air soldering.

DON'T

- **DON'T** inadvertently short something because you are not paying attention with your probes or forgot a screw or tool on the board.
- **DON'T** inject more power than necessary to identify a short. Start low (.5V) and if needed, increase slowly but never exceed safe limits.
- **DON'T** inject power to find a very small partial short. It would take too much voltage for something to get hot (Ohm's law).
- **DON'T** clean up your flux residues while the board is very hot to prevent thermal shock.
- **DON'T** power up your board, or test components if it is still hot after soldering a component.

- **DON'T** inadvertently reflow chips that should not be reflowed unless absolutely necessary, such as SMC. Always avoid CPU GPU reflow.

- **DON'T** heat around your RAM, CPU, GPU, PCH.

- **DON'T** use hot air near any plastic, especially connectors. If possible, use hot tweezers or soldering iron.

- **DON'T** inverse your probes when testing for resistance. <u>Black probe always on ground</u>. if you invert them you can incorrectly measure low resistance even if there is no short.

- **DON'T** inhale flux fumes. Use fume extractor or at a minimum a fan to direct fumes away from you. Gloves recommended.

- **DON'T** power right away early 2015 A1534's after a repair. Use USB-A to USB-C connector to supply 5v first until you hear a chime. Failure to do this may kill your board. All 1534 have a battery off button as the connector is under the logic board.

TROUBLESHOOTING FUNDAMENTALS

A good way to approach no power issues is to divide the power system in three sections.

LAYER 1: POWER SOURCE

Do I have good DC IN from charger and a good battery? Can these two power sources communicate correctly with the computer? If you have a known good charge port put it on to eliminate a potential charge port issues.

LAYER 2: MACBOOK CORE POWER MANAGEMENT: PP3V42_G3H AND PPBUS RAILS

These two rails are essentials to provide power to every component in the MacBook. As they interact with external power sources and battery there is a little more to know about them compared to other rails.

LAYER 3: ALL THE OTHER DOWNSTREAM POWER RAILS GETTING POWER FROM PPBUS

If everything is good up to layer 3, it means the core power management system of the MacBook is working fine and the problem is likely related to a downstream rail receiving power from PPBUS. In the next section we'll explain how to test voltage on these rails in a systematic and logical way.

FINAL SYSTEM CHECK: ALL_SYS_PWRGD

When all the power rails are good, SMC will receive ALL_SYS_PWRGD and get the process in motion to create the last power rail CPU VCORE. If CPU does not turn on, check this signal first.

TROUBLESHOOTING SEQUENCE

STEP ONE: DO A READING AT THE CHARGING PORT

Use an AMP meter with USB-C MacBook or a modified MagSafe cable connected to a bench power supply. Disconnect the battery before doing this test. The amp meter reading can give you a lot of useful information. For example if voltage is correct eg 20V then the PP3Vx rail is working (as well as the CD3215s on USB-C MacBooks). If Amperage is low eg .1 amp, the problem could very well be a short on PPBUS. Of course the problem may also be due to the charger or charge port itself. Refer to Repair wiki to learn what different amp reading means on different models.

STEP TWO: REMOVE THE BOARD AND DO A MINUTIA VISUAL INSPECTION.

When we say minutia we mean it. With time you can do it faster but if you are new to the field it is very easy to miss a small clue and wasting a lot of time troubleshooting when you don't have to. <u>You must find a visual clue if any exists;</u> it's the fastest way to wrap up a repair. Make sure you lay your eyes on every single component on the board. It will take you less than 5 minutes; with experience less than 2. Look for traces of corrosion, water marks, very slight component discoloration, cracks, bulges, dark/dull vs shinny terminals. If dealing with prior repair, add looking for missing components, solder bridges, any kind of poor workmanship.

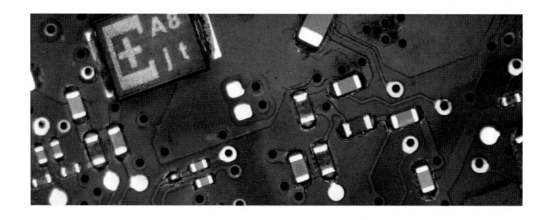

STEP THREE: IDENTIFY THE PROBLEMATIC POWER RAIL STARTING WITH THE G3H RAILS

Voltage test. The problematic rail is either not receiving voltage, not the proper voltage, or voltage on only part of the rail. Again we start with the most important rails PPBUS and PP3V42. If PPBUS is there at the proper voltage no need to test PP3V42 as PPBUS cannot get to proper voltage without the SMC which is powered by PP3V42. Make sense? If any rail is missing or low voltage, test for short. If no short check rail creation dependencies (enable signals, feedback loops, etc).

IF THE G3H RAILS ARE OK, WE MOVE OUR ATTENTION TO THE DOWNSTREAM RAILS (S5 TO S0 RAILS)

If the G3H rails are fine, then the problem is with the downstream rails. Before you go any further you will need to open up the schematic and go to the power alias page to identify all the power rails so you can test them.

Remember these rules:

1) The board powers up in sequence starting with S5 rails (power off), then S4 rails (hibernate), S3 rails (sleep) and finally S0 rails (power on).
2) <u>All rails for a given state must be on</u> for the next state to start powering on.

Based on these rules, if any S0 rail has voltage, don't waste time checking voltage on S3, S4 or S5 rails, they're on! If you have at least one S4 rail, no need to check any S5 rails etc. It's important to understand this concept. It will save you a lot of time.

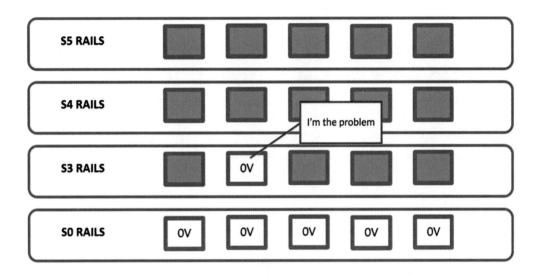

The best method to troubleshoot downstream rails is to identify the lowest state where there is at least one rail with proper voltage. So you start with S0 rails and start testing the voltage on those rails. If none of them has voltage, you move up to S3 rails. Let say, the first one you check has voltage. What can you conclude? You can conclude that S5 and S4 rails are fine, the problem is likely another S3 rail and it is usually the case. There are exceptions to this but this rule generally applies. Here's an example with a S3 rail missing.

Let say all S3 rails have proper voltage except one. We then turn the power off and test for short.
If a rail does not come on and you think it should, check the rail trigger, enable signal.

The state trigger signals are:

S5 STATE	SMC_PM_G2_EN / PM_SLP_SUS_L
S4 STATE	PM_SLP_5_L
S3 STATE	PM_SLP_4_L
S0 STATE	PM_SLP_S3_L
VCORE	ALL_SYS_PWRGD

ALL_SYS_PWRGD will verify the following rails before releasing its signal: PP1V8_S3, PP5V_S3, PP1V2_S3, PP1V05_S0, PP5V_S0, PP3V3_S0, PP1V5_S0. If any of these S3 or S0 rails malfunctions, it will pull down ALL_SYS_PWRGD and terminate the power-on process.

IF A MISSING RAIL IS NOT SHORTED, NOT WATER DAMAGED, THEN TROUBLESHOOTING IS A LITTLE MORE INVOLVING.

Where is this rail created? What is required to create this rail? Are these conditions met? If all the conditions are met and the chip or power regulator responsible is not delivering this voltage then this chip is likely bad (unless it is not making proper contact with the board).

Whether we are troubleshooting a power rail, a chip or a state, if we are not dealing with a short or visual damage, the process is always the same. We need to review the "creation process" of what we are investigating to identify what is not happening as it should. At the end of this book there are a series of reference charts to help you get familiar with the requirements for key chip, rail and state to turn on.

Chasing a fault not related to a short or liquid damage is definitely more involving but the right attitude is to see these challenges as fun puzzles to be solved. Fortunately, most cases are not like this.

Sometimes you may face a situation where all the lines for a given state are present and the next state is not powering on, what's going on? Like ICs, states (S5 to S0) also have trigger enable signals. If all lines are there and the next state is not powering on, you must investigate the state enable signal the same way you would investigate the enable signal for a chip.

DEALING WITH CORROSION

Beyond the obvious risk of causing shorts and component failures, water damage affects the conductivity of soldered components and traces. Is it fair to assume that any visible signs of corrosion must be removed or it will continue to damage the board over time. Corrosion creates internal resistance or worse, opens the line. Before resorting to ultrasonic cleaning, the following steps can pretty well fix the corrosion issues and solve the problem:

1. Clean the corroded area with isopropyl alcohol and brush off all visible surface corrosion with a toothbrush.
2. Apply flux and gently heat the area.
3. If corrosion remains, use an old iron to gently scrape it off (with flux of course).
4. After cleaning, re-thin all pads and contact points showing previous signs of corrosion.
5. With Boarview, identify where each of the corroded point was going or coming from and test for connectivity. If there is no connectivity and you can't revive the pad, you may have to run a wire between these points and apply solder mask to ensure you are not shorting other components in the process.
6. Identify potential corrosion under chips by tilting the board to be able to see under the chip. For most chips (excluding CPU /GPU/RAM/ NANDs/PCH) reflowing affected chips may very well solve the problem by burning the junk causing contact issues. This is often the case with 5V issues due to water damaged CD3215.

SHORTS TO GROUND

Short to ground affects everything on that rail not only the faulty component. It can also affect other rails if a gate between rails is broken (eg blown Mosfets). There are two ways to identify the component causing the short. If the visual inspection leads you to suspect a component (discoloration etc), you can test the internal resistance of the component and its resistance to ground. Always make sure the MacBook is disconnected from power before testing for resistance. If resistance is lower than spec and this weird looking component has a path to ground it is likely the source of the problem. Replace and retest.

If the visual inspection did not provide any clue and the diagnostic has confirmed a short to ground then the best approach is to inject voltage on that rail and see which component gets hot fast. See voltage injection. There is a third option that we won't cover here as it requires a high precision 4-digit multimeter which can detect tiny resistance variations.

If the voltage on a rail is much lower than should be it is usually due to a short and you will be able to identify it by injecting voltage most of the time. Be aware though that faulty resistors or an "active short", meaning a short that is only present when there is voltage on the rail, can also cause a voltage drop. While uncommon you don't wish for an active short: you can't confirm the presence of such a short as you can't measure resistance when power is on.

- **ALWAYS DISCONNECT POWER BEFORE TESTING FOR SHORT TO GROUND**
  (resistance mode with black probe on ground).

- **ANYTHING BELOW 1 OHM IS A DEFINITIVE SHORT.**
  Above 1 ohm it depends on the normal resistance of that rail.

- **COILS ARE A GOOD PLACE TO TEST FOR SHORTS.**
  Except for CPU / GPU, you expect 100K ohms+ resistance on all rails.

- **SHORTS TO GROUND ARE TYPICALLY CAUSED BY CAPACITORS AND ICS** and less often by MOSFETS when they have a path to ground.

- The other passive components, resistors, filters, coils don't short to ground for the simple reason that they don't have a path to ground; they carry voltage on "the high side".

- Typically, only one component will be shorted; you just need to find it, usually with voltage injection.

- Mosfets don't typically short to ground but rather develop an internal short (they become a wire) letting whatever voltage IN become voltage OUT. Shorted Mosfets also carry the "short to ground" across the rails connected to the Mosfet.

- If a Mosfet or a power regulator is defective and allows high voltage to flow though, components may get hot or defective as a result without being shorted to ground. An internally shorted Mosfet can damage ICs and power regulators on that line, even the CPU. It's always good practice to replace BGA chips that have received improper voltage as well as any Mosfet connected to a shorted component.

VOLTAGE INJECTION

The charging circuit is typically smart enough to know there is a short somewhere and reduce power preventing identifying the component responsible for the short when the charger is plugged in. For this reason, we can't usually use the charger and we must inject voltage directly on the troubled rail to find the component responsible for the short. We do this by soldering temporary testing wires on the board and connecting them to an external power supply.

With voltage injection, it's usually easy to find the fault as the culprit is typically the hottest component on that rail as short to ground implies high amperage and high heat. To find the faulty "hot" component you can use your fingers, alcohol, lighter gas, freeze spray, upside down compressed air can or a thermal imager. Remember the faulty component is the one getting abnormally hot first. For good measure I must mention that It is also possible to identify shorted components with high precision and rather expense four-digit multimeters but these are not commonly used.

- When Injecting voltage you control the voltage, not the amp!
- Always stay well below the normal voltage for that rail.
- As a general rule, no need to ever go above 3V and/or 2 amp to find something getting hot.
- Find a good size component to solder your positive lead to: a coil, a fuse, or the positive lead of a large cap. The ground can be anchored on any screw hole.
- Set your amp to the max and voltage to .5V then power on and slowly increase voltage until something gets hot. Pay attention to ensure no large BGA is heating up such as CPU, GPU, PCH.

- When injecting PPBUS never exceed voltage of downstream rails if you are not 100% sure the downstream Mosfets are good.
- Small partial shorts may be difficult to diagnose with this method as you would need to inject too much voltage to generate enough amp for something to get hot (Ohms law).
- **VCORE/CPU** always appears shorted because they have very low resistance to ground. This being said, if VCORE is less than 1 ohm, it is shorted and the CPU is dead.
- After replacing a shorted component, injecting voltage on that rail should show close to zero amp. Success!

PPBUS FULL VS PARTIAL SHORT WARNING

- If PPBUS is fully shorted (less than .5 ohm), it is safe to inject voltage without checking downstream coils.
- If PPBUS is partially shorted IT IS NOT SAFE TO INJECT VOLTAGE before you known if the problem is on PPBUS or a downstream rail. Let's assume the problem comes from a downstream rail such as VCORE, injecting voltage on PPBUS would flow directly to VCORE (CPU) and kill the board!
- In the previous example, what looked like a partial PPBUS short was not a short to ground at all. A blown Mosfet has turned into a wire connecting PPBUS directly to the VCORE rail. VCORE has a naturally lower resistance to ground, so PPBUS is showing the same low resistance.
- To confirm if a blown Mosfet is causing the "partial short" reading on PPBUS, try to find a downstream rail with a similar reading eg 50 ohms. When you find one, confirm both rails are really connected by checking resistance across both rails (eg between the downstream coil and the PPBUS fuse). If it is close to 0 ohm the MOSFET is blown and that's why PPBUS appears

to be partially shorted. Replace the Mosfet and the "false short" on PPBUS should be gone.

- When PPBUS has a "real partial short" PPBUS resistance to ground will be lower than the resistance between both rails. This makes sense because the Mosfets are doing their job and maintaining high resistance between the rails.
- If you suspect a downstream Mosfet to be bad, especially CPU Mosfets, fix or remove it before injecting voltage on PPBUS.
- Once it is confirmed that the short is isolated to PPBUS, you can safely inject voltage.
- When diagnosing the source of a short, sometimes it is useful to isolate the supply from the load side of a given rail. You do so by lifting one side of the coil or fuse. For example, you can remove PPBUS fuses F7000/7001 to see if a PPBUS short comes from the ISL supply side or one of the downstream rails. It could also help troubleshoot low PPBUS voltage situations to see if voltage becomes stable again when the other rails are disconnected from PPBUS.

RESISTANCE AND DIODE MEASUREMENTS

RESISTANCE TESTING

For MacBook diagnosis, we primarily use resistance/continuity testing to identify rails shorted to ground, test passive components and identify broken traces. Always ensure the board is powered off before testing for resistance.

- Black probe always on GND, if you turn the probes around the resistance reading may be incorrect.
- If there is 0Ω reading between a rail and GND or a reading below 1Ω there is definitely a short.
- If the reading shows a non-zero value, whether there is a short depends on the normal resistance for that rail. Typically high amperage rail = low resistance such as CPU / GPU rails.
- Don't expect precise ohm measurements for high ohm resistors eg 100K ohms resistors.
- Resistance at VCORE should be at least 1 ohm;

DIODE VS OHMS TESTING

Diode mode does essentially the same thing but instead of using ohms it measures voltage drop across two points as a way to infer its resistance. Smaller the number, lower is the resistance.

- Diode Mode offers two advantages over resistance testing. It is way faster and it makes it easy to compare results against a series of known good values. This is especially useful when the problem is hard to find and you have to check dozens of lines to try to identify what could be wrong such as testing each line on a connector.

- Good diode readings on MacBooks are often between 0.4V and 0.6V (400 to 600) but not always.
- Diode values close to zero eg .06V means there is very low resistance to ground and possibly a short.
- For rails that are naturally low resistance / high current, resistance measurement is better (less than 20 ohms or .05V diode).
- When testing diodes either in diode or ohm modes, you should get a good reading in one direction and O/L in the other.

SPECIAL CASE 1: CURRENT SENSING RESISTORS

- Many ICs have current sensing circuits to detect if the power supplied to the chip is out of whack. If it is, or if the sensing circuit is malfunctioning the IC shuts down.

- The sensing circuit is a loop going from the IC up to the voltage rail and back to the IC. There will be a resistor directly on the voltage rail between the lines and also one resistor on each line going to the IC for a total of 3 resistors in the loop. Here's an example of a current sensing circuit. R7021 and R7022 each have a line going to the IC. The IC analyzes the difference in voltage between the two lines and determines if it is normal. If it is not normal, it shuts down the output.

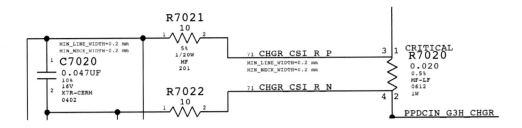

- A simple way to test the sensing circuit is to <u>add the values of the three resistors</u> (eg 100 + 100 + 500 ohms = 700 ohms) and compare with the resistance where the loop attaches to the IC. If the resistance does not match, identify the bad resistor and replace it. If you don't want to do the math, simply check each resistor resistance to ensure they are within specs.

- IC Feedback loops work in a similar way. Instead of testing the input voltage it tests the output via a similar loop on the IC voltage output line. If you suspect a bad feedback loop, check the resistors as you would do on a sensing loop.

SPECIAL CASE 2: DROP DOWN RESISTORS

- Sometimes the voltage going to an IC is "dropped down" from the source voltage such as ACIN on ISL charging chips.

- The voltage is dropped down by placing two resistors between the input voltage rail and ground; the IC is connected in the middle. In this case R7010 and R7011 are dropping down the voltage going to ACIN.

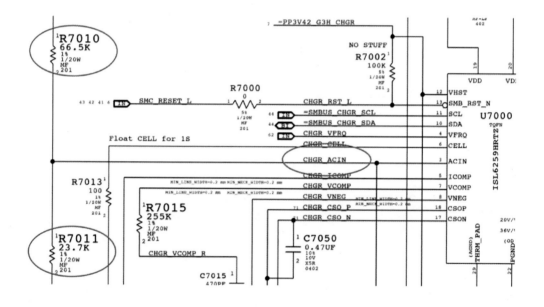

- To confirm that the resistors are delivering the proper voltage you simply divide the value of the resistor connected to ground by the sum of both resistors and multiply the result by the source voltage. For example if the resistor connected to ground is 100K ohms and the other resistor connected to the voltage rail is 300K ohms then 100K / (100K + 300K) = 25%. If source voltage is 12V, the drop down voltage should be 3V (25% * 12V).

- If source voltage is good and you don't want to do the math, simply check each resistor resistance to ensure they are within specs. Generally though we usually start by testing the resulting voltage and only if it's out of whack do we investigate the resistors.

COMPONENT TESTING

TESTING MOSFETS

- The dot on Mosfets indicates pin 1 of 3 of the source pins. The gate is typically pin 4. The other 4 pins are drain. Note that pins numbers are always going counter clockwise on any chip.
- There should be high resistance (ohm) between gate, source and drain - test all the combinations.
- In diode mode you should have around .5v between source and drain in one direction and OL in the other.
- Test if the gate opens when it should. P Mosfet: gate voltage needs to be lower than source to open, N Mosfet: gate voltage needs to be equal of higher. You can often identify the type of Mosfet by the last chip digit: even = P, odd = N.
- **The three tests above are the typical tests to confirm if a Mosfet is good.** Below are more details on how to conduct these tests and fix gate activation if it happens while testing.
- With no power, the gate should be off (discharged) and you want it that way for testing. It may happen that you inadvertently activate the gate by misplacing the probes or touching the gate with your finger – see fix below.
- **To check resistance with Gate:**
  P Mosfet (**red probe on gate**) N Mosfet (**black probe on gate**).
  If you reverse the probes, you will turn the Gate ON and you then have low resistance between Source and Gate.

- Resistance check between Source and Gate is tricky as there is often a resistor between them as mentioned previously and you end up measuring the resistance of that resistor. If resistance is lower than the resistor value either the resistor is defective or "Source to Gate" is shorted.

- **WHAT TRIGGERS / OPENS THE GATE**
  N Mosfet (**red probe on gate, black on source**)
  P Mosfet (**red probe on source, black on gate**)

- **HOW TO CLOSE / DISCHARGE THE GATE**
  N Mosfet (**red probe on source, black on gate**)
  P Mosfet (**red probe on gate, black on source**)

PASSIVE COMPONENTS

CAPACITORS (C)

Typical fault: Internally Shorted (close to zero ohms between sides). This results in a short to ground as capacitors typically have one pad on ground. If you measure low resistance to ground, remember that all capacitors wired in parallel will appear shorted; not only the faulty one. Voltage injection is usually the best way of identifying the culprit. If voltage injection is not an option, you can remove the capacitors on the shorted rail and test them off circuit for internal short. A healthy capacitor will show lower resistance initially and climb up during resistance testing. If the resistance does not climb up the capacitor is bad. Sometimes a fully charged capacitor may appear shorted. Best to wait a little after unplugging the charger to prevent a false reading. If you want to be 100% sure, do a capacitance test off circuit.

RESISTORS (R)

Typical fault: actual resistance value falls outside of tolerance thresholds (too high or two low). Test your resistors with resistance or diode mode (DM) measurement; DM = with red probe on ground).

COIL/INDUCTOR (L)

Typical fault: they become open (but they rarely fail). Inductors are just coiled wires. Test in resistance mode. Expect low resistance.

FUSE (F) & FILTERS

Typical fault: they can become open. Test in resistance mode. Expect low resistance. Filters, capacitors and ceramic coils often look similar; ceramic coils typically have more of a square shape where capacitors and filters have more of a rectangular shape.

DIODES (D)

Typical fault: when they fail they either become close in both directions or fully open in both directions. Diodes often have a mark on the cathode side (the output).The quick and dirty test is to check resistance in both directions. You should get a reading in one direction and OL in the other. Now the proper test is diode mode with power turned off of course. The meter will display the voltage drop across the diode. The voltage drop varies: normal diodes 0.6–0.7 V, Schottky diodes 0.3–0.5 V and LEDs from 1–4 V. Probe direction matters as current is only supposed to flow in one direction with diodes. If you measure 0.3 V or less, then your diode has likely shorted. When measured with probes inverted there should be open or very high resistance if the diode is good.

MACBOOK DISSASEMBLY

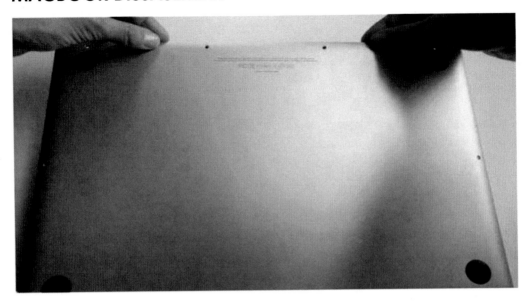

Most logic board repairs require removing the board. There are an abundance of guides on the internet on how to remove back cover / logic boards on different models (e.g. ifixit). Just google your model before starting.

Before attempting a logic board removal:

1. Make sure you have a proper way to organize removed screws and components to facilitate reassembly. A magnetic board can be very helpful in this regard.
2. Take pictures along the way to help you with reassembly.
3. Make sure you reinstall screws at the proper place, especially long screws which can damage the board or other components.
4. It's very easy to damage something when disconnecting connectors, including the connectors themselves and their ribbons. Also pay attention to nearby components easily ripped off the board.
5. If you ever need to remove antenna cables near the screen hinges, when reassembly make sure not to pinch any under a screw and pay attention to reinsert them correctly in their respective grooves.

MACBOOK REPAIR FUNDAMENTALS

TYPICAL REPAIRS INVOLVE:

- Removing, and usually replacing, faulty components
- Cleaning / removing corrosion
- Reflowing components
- Addressing failed traces between components by either rebuilding the traces and probe points with solder or via jumper wires.

WORKING WITH HEAT

- Always clean flux residues even it is says clean free. Don't wait too long after repair to remove it (it will become hard) but don't remove it when it's blazing hot either.
- There are three variables to soldering perfection: the flux, the heat and the tip. If something is not working as you expect, the issue is one of these three things, when in doubt just add flux☺.
- **FLUX** Don't underestimate the importance of working with fresh clean flux at all times. Flux oxidizes and dissipates quickly under heat. If the flux starts changing color, it's time to clean up. Every soldering job works better with freshly applied flux. Many simple repairs require a few flux "switchovers": initial wicking, thinning, chip installation, etc.
- Every iron/ hot air station is different. 350 may mean 320 on one iron and 370 on another. Your best guide is your feel and your eyes. If it's not melting fast enough, increase heat, if it seems too hot, bring it down. When set correctly, you rarely change iron temperature, you simply adjust tip sizes.
- Before wicking pads, apply leaded solder over lead free solder to reduce the solder melting point and facilitate solder removal. This method (applying led solder) also works to speed up component removal especially for those with large anchor pads such as tantalum capacitors.

- Move the iron towards the end of the braid rope not toward the spool in order to retain heat. Periodically remove sections that have been used as they will attract heat and reduce the braid effectiveness.
- When cleaning pads, make sure to lift-up the iron and braid at the same time. Otherwise, you will solder the braid to the pads and risk ripping them off.
- Do not apply any pressure when "wicking" solder; you can easily pull pads and that's definitely the kind of problems you want to avoid.

WORKING WITH THE SOLDERING IRON

- You want the soldering tip hot enough to melt the solder efficiently, but excess heat is unnecessary and can reduce the lifespan of the tip big time. For example, increasing the average iron temperature from 350°C to 400°C will reduce the iron tip life by half.
- Setting your (real) iron temperature to 350C is a good starting point for most jobs.
- Stay away from rounded tips, one or two small size bevel tips and flat tips is all you need.
- Always match iron tip to pad size. If the tip is too small, melting is difficult, too big and you risk bridging across pads.
- The "go to" repair solder 63/37 (leaded) melts at exactly **183C.** Lead-free solder melts gradually starting at **217C.**
- You may want to use these melting points to calibrate your iron if you don't have a thermocouple.
- Ribbon cable repair eg Flexgate: lower **260C** temperature is safer.

WORKING WITH HOT AIR

- The distance between the air gun and the surface has a bigger impact on temperature than the actual heat setting. After warming up the board somewhat, try to work very close to the chip.
- Choosing proper heat and airflow is a balancing act. Usually the faster you can remove and install components the better; it reduces the risk of causing significant heat buildup in the board and transferring heat to other components.
- You have to achieve this goal without exceeding the heat limit of different chips; some ICs are more susceptible to high heat than others but usually the faster you can get out of there the better. As a general rule, if it takes more than 15 to 20 seconds to remove a chip, there is not enough heat or airflow. Of course the bigger the chip the more heat it takes to achieve the same result. This applies to board thickness too.
- You can probably remove a 0201 capacitor in 5 seconds @ 320C but need 400C or more for 20 seconds to remove an SMC.
- 380°- 420°C is a good place to start. Lower heat for small components, higher heat for bigger chips. 4MM is a good all-around tip. You may require bigger ones for big chips.
- When removing chips go for max air to speed up the process. When installing chips go for low air to prevent the component from flying off. When the component is at least partially soldered down you should finish with higher air flow; surface tension should now hold the component safely on the board.
- If it takes a long time to remove a chip you may have missed the presence of underfill. STOP before damaging the board! Scrape it off at low heat then proceed to remove the chip.
- Take time to properly protect surrounding areas from heat. It only takes a few seconds and can save your board. This includes the underside right under the repair area (use some form of metal box such as an old hard drive as a heat sink). On

the working surface you can use Kapton tape or a thin metal shield of some sort to protect nearby components.

- If exposing plastics is unavoidable (eg working near a connector), you can wrap those plastic components with a couple layers of aluminum foil with an excess "tail" of foil coming off of the area.
- Always try to direct airflow away from sensitive components surrounding the repair. Don't work in an uncomfortable position, always take the time to rotate the board to ensure you can do your best work.
- Make sure your BGA chip does not move around when flowing or you will mess up the balls – reduce your air flow. Also if your BGA chip is swimming in a thick sea of flux it will have a tendency to fly off; only apply a thin coat of flux before installing your BGA chip.
- Generally you want to heat the area until you have some visual indications that the underside is wetting, and you see the chip moving into place. You can gently tap the chip from the side to confirm it is wiggling and going back into place.
- After soldering a chip, it's good practice to finish up by cleaning the exposed pins with your iron.

- **PREVENT SMALL COMPONENTS FROM FLYING OFF.**

  Hold your smaller components down with tweezers while applying hot air; make sure to hold the component from the top so the bottom is free to makes good contact with the pads. You can also preheat the pads with hot air to reduce the time required for surface tension to take over when you install the component (less time applying air = less risk that the chip flies off).

- **TO FLUX OR NOT TO FLUX.** It is generally preferable to use flux when removing components with hot air but it is not 100% necessary. If you want to reuse the component, especially large ones, then use flux. When you want to be extra careful in limiting heat to adjacent components you may decide not use flux as flux flows around and carries heat with it. Not using flux tends to limit the heat to whatever is under the gun.

- In the rare cases where you can attempt soldering without removing the logic board (risky), make sure the screen is folded open and out of the way.
- If the chip you are attempting to remove has underfill or rubber compound such as SMCs, apply low heat eg 100C and carefully scrape if off first.

BGA CHIPS

- If you're going to be replacing a BGA chip with a replacement that comes pre-balled, it's best to air solder the chip directly on cleaned pads rather than rethined pads. The balls it comes with is all that's required to anchor the chip securely on the board.
- Inspect the pads. If there are exposed trace on the board don't reinstall the chip before covering the traces with UV curing solder mask – the green stuff and curing it properly. If you don't, the new solder balls will go there. If a pad is missing (can happen due to wicking action), it may be a "no stuff" pad as they are not anchored to anything and easily ripped off. If it's a real pad, then you have to rebuild it with a coiled jumping wire or repair pads made for this. In both cases you will have to apply solder mask to hold the wire down and prevent shorting with other pads. If you face such an issue take the time to see a few video on how it's done.
- If you are reinstalling a chip, whether you will be reballing it or not, the first step is to apply a thin coat of leaded solder over the lead-free balls. That will help with wicking it clean or reinstalling it as is.
- If your chip moved a little while heating it, use your air gun to direct the chip where it needs to go. If you're happy with the chip position, keep the air flow pretty much dead center from the top making tight circles to prevent pushing the chip of the pads.
- For typical BGA chips with balls everywhere, once wetted, wiggle the chip around with your tweezers to ensure good contact. If balls are only around the chip (not in the middle), then after an initial heating, reheat it a second time while applying some soft pressure from the top to help the chip sit well, then remove hot air while maintaining that soft pressure for a few more seconds. Finally, flux the chip again and drag a small iron tip around it to remove any excess solder.

- When can you stop heating the chip? Watch the exposed lead of your component and eventually you'll see the solder change from solid to liquid. Give it a couple seconds past that point. If you're targeting a component that doesn't have visible solder then watch the solder of the components around it - once they're uniformly in a shiny, liquid phase, then the BGA chip is likely properly soldered already or very soon.
- Finally, remove heat from the board gradually by expanding the circles with your air gun for 5-10 seconds to be sure that the board's is gradually cooling down.

TO WICK OR NOT TO WICK

Let's start with the ideal scenario: a BGA chip with fresh and evenly sized solder balls installed on an absolutely clean wicked flat surface. That's ideal but not absolutely necessary. What you want is for each ball to connect to the board so as long as things are pretty much even on both sides, it can theoretically work. Generally, it is good practice to wick away existing lead free solder from the board to make the surface flat.

You really have two options: either you wick the board clean or at a minimum, thin over existing solder before applying the replacement component. For small components simply thinning the pads with leaded solder will do. In the case of BGA chips, or connectors, you can attempt either way. Whatever you decide, make sure the resulting surface is relatively flat. On iPhones, it's good practice NOT to wick BGA pads; too much risk of pulling pads of the board. Just evenly thin the pads with leaded solder then install the new chip.

REBALL WITH SOLDER PASTE

- Dry the solder paste by rubbing it in paper towel before using.
- Put a little flux on the bga chip and spread it thinly with a brush. Never apply flux on the stencil or solder may stick to it.
- The name of the game is to ensure that once the chip and the stencil are lined up properly nothing moves. There are many ways to do this; some use jigs, others tweezers, others even use heat resistant glass such as a galaxy phone lens to press the stencil on the chip. Whatever works as long as nothing moves.
- 280C to 300C is good for solder paste. Start from far away taking your time to slowly heat the chip. As you approach, make smaller and smaller circles towards the chip. A slow melting process ensures a better outcome. Sometimes it takes two or three attempts to achieve a good reball, even for pro, so don't despair if it does not work on the first attempt.
- To remove the stencil, there are different approaches. Some heat the stencil at 100C with high air flow. Other poke at some stubborn pins with tweezers.
- If some balls seem really stuck on the stencil, apply flux directly on the stencil this time and reheat.
- Once the stencil is removed, it's good practice to reflow the balls once more before reinstalling (to make then perfectly round).
- If after completing the process a ball is missing, no worries. Add a tiny drop of flux and carefully place a solder ball of proper diameter in the missing spot. Melt slowly with low heat/low air.

OTHER BGA TIPS

- Squared hole stencils are easier to work with than rounded ones (less surface for solder to stick to).
- To stay fresh, solder paste must be stored in the fridge.

WORKING WITHOUT STENCILS

While it's always preferable to install a chip with "fresh" solder balls, you can attempt to install a chip from a donor board without reballing it with the following method:

- Thoroughly clean the logic board pads (wick). Apply hot air if necessary to help with the process.
- Carefully thin each ball of the replacement BGA, aiming for good evenness (critical).
- If wicking pads is not desirable (eg iPhone) then thin the receiving pads evenly.

BGA REHEAT VS REFLOW

Reheating chips (low heat eg 200C) can help kill corrosion / conductive dirt under the chip causing shorts. Reflow (high heat) helps fix poor solder joints. These two approaches solve different problems. Most chips can be reheated when necessary but not all chips can be reflown without risk. An ultrasonic cleaner addresses the same problem as reheating chips: remove junk causing improper connections; it does not fix bad solder joints (cold joints).

REPAIRING DAMAGED TRACES AND PADS

If a trace or a pad in no longer conducting voltage, you must repair it by soldering a jumper wire across it. We typically use shielded copper wires for this. Use an appropriate diameter wire for the repair. You simply scrape off / burn off the extremities to ensure good contact. Once the wire is thinned and soldered down, the extra length can simply be removed by carefully wiggling it with your tweezers. You can also rebuild a pad with copper wire by coiling it or simply buy premade replacement pads. Solder mask is typically applied to glue the wire down and isolate it from other voltage contacts. Note that solder mask will harden with UV light (look away to protect your eyes).

DEALING WITH SHIELDS (mostly an iPhone thing)

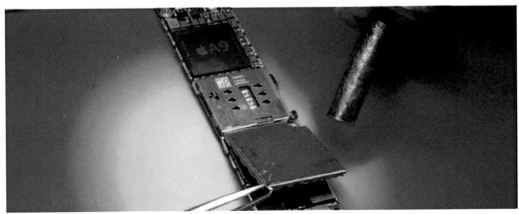

To remove shields go for high heat, high air, big nozzle (MAX everything) for IPhone 6 and below. Hold the shield with tweezers and let the board drop. To reinstall you can add flux and tack the sides of the shield with the iron. For iPhone 7-8, also go for high everything but first scrape the one side with rubber. You also will have to apply gentle pressure to separate the shield from the board as it will not drop by itself. For newer phones with split boards you need to perforate carefully all around the shield to weaken the bond without dislodging components inside the shield, and then you pick a corner and pry the shield up, no heat necessary and no need to put the shields back on these phones.

REPLACING CONNECTORS

- Two methods to install connectors: wick the board if you have enough working space, if not just thin all pads except ground planes. You will apply solder directly to the ground planes later.
- Make sure there is lots of flux before thinning connector pads. If you don't, you will melt the connector.
- Remove with more heat, Install with less heat.
  eg If you REMOVE @ 350C 40% air, INSTALL @ 300C 20% air.
- Using a hot plate at 200C makes the process easier (wicking, removing, installing).
- New connectors take all the heat as there is no board to absorb some of it.
- Wicking the pads ensures the connector lays flat / makes good contact with all the pins. Tack some pins down with a small iron

tip and finish ground pins with a large iron tip or hot air (be careful).

- One method to install new connectors: hold the connector down with tweezers and dips iron tip in solder paste to solder each pin or at least a few anchor pins (paste allows for one hand operation). Finish ground pins by applying new solder either with iron or hot air.

REPAIRING FLEX CABLE

- Many boards from the USB-C era have suffered from "flex gate" where the screen would turn off when adjusting the angle of the screen.
- Apple has honored some flex gate warranties, your mileage may vary.
- The simplest fix is to change the screen assembly (expensive). Many expert technicians have elected to splice the defective cable with a donor cable. This is being achieved by carefully removing the protective shield on both ribbons where the connection will be made, thinning the lines and connecting them with jumping wires. This is a complex repair. I recommend you watch this video if entertaining this repair yourself.
https://youtu.be/5nBiN8Uujlw

ULTRASONIC LOGIC BOARD CLEANING

- An ultrasonic cleaner is not absolutely necessary in your repair arsenal and many repair shops don't have one. They serve two functions: a general cleaning function: remove gunk, flux, dirt and some surface corrosion. They may also bring a dead board back to life if the issue pertained to junk causing faulty connections under ICs. Note that reheating a chip (vs reflowing) usually achieves the same fix.

- Try to repair and bring the board back to life before cleaning. If you cannot fix it 100%, at least make notes of problem areas before cleaning as you may lose visual clues of where the problems were.
- While ultrasonic cleaning can often solve board problems when the issue is electrical bridges/shorts due to corrosion or debris, cleaning won't do anything if the issues pertain to badly corroded solder joints (cold joints).
- Use pure water (not tap), proper cleaning liquid made for PCB boards and respect minimal liquid levels in the tank.
- When using a new batch of liquid, degauss for at least 15 minutes to prevent board damage.
- With proper temp (50-60C) no more than 2 min per side.

- Yes, remove thermal compound before putting the board in the cleaner as well as any sticky soft shields / tape.
- When practical, remove any metal shields that are covering components to ensure those get cleaned as well.
- Soak the cleaned board in IPA before drying.
- Make sure the board is 100% dry before testing it. You can help accelerate the process with compressed air, low temp oven, low hot air or simply give it time but beware those areas under shields can trap moisture.
- Glossy vs. matte finish boards. Boards that appear to have a "glossy" finish are more delicate & fragile than boards that appear to have a "matte" finish. Clean glossy boards for one minute per side. Affected Apple models include A1989, A1990.

RISK OF BOARD DEATH FROM ULTRASONIC CLEANING

A working board can be killed by an ultrasonic cleaner. Common causes of death are:

- Cleaning at too high a temperature.
- Cleaning the board for too long.
- Trying to power the board before it is fully dry.
- Using inappropriate cleaning materials that are too rough on the board.

WHERE TO GO FROM HERE

We hope this introduction to logic board repair helped you develop a good understanding of basic troubleshooting and repair methods. Such an introductory guide can't cover all situations nor all board variations. We invite you to consult additional freely available resources such as repair.wiki and logi.wiki for board specific troubleshooting information.

ADDENDUM

QUICK REFERENCE CHARTS

SECTION ONE: KEY POWER RAILS

	REQUIRED	FROM	TO	Notes & Examples
PP3V3 (USB-C)	PM_EN_P3V3_G3H	ISL	3.3V Buck Converter	
	PP3V3_G3H_RTC	ISL	3.3V Buck Converter	U6990
PP3V42 (MAGSAFE)	PPVIN_G3H	Charge port	3.42V Buck Converter	U7090
	SHDN	P3V42_SHDN	U7090	Voltage sense
	3.42V	U7090	ISL/U7090	
	SMC_BC_ACOK	SMC	U7090	From ISL (CHGR_OK) To SMC_BC_ACOK
	SYS_ONEWIRE	SMC	ISL/U7000	
	ADAPTOR SENSE	U7000	green light	SYS_ONEWIRE becomes ADAPTOR SENSE
PPBUS	DCIN /ACIN	--	ISL	ACIN not lower than 3.4V/3.9V pro
	CHGR_ACOK	ISL	SMC	(ISL) CHGR_ACOK = (SMC) SMC_BC_ACOK
	VDD/VDDP	ISL	ISL (5v)	Feedback loop
	SMC_RESET_L	ISL/RESET CHIP	SMC	PPBUS & 20V from charger
	SMBUS	SMC	ISL	Boost PPBUS +.2v to proper voltage
	Q7030/40	ISL	PPBUS_G3H	
20 VOLT CHGR	PP3V3_G3H	ISL	SMC (VBAT)	PP3V3 or PP3V42 depending on model
	DCIN /ACIN	--	ISL	ACIN minimum 3.4V/3.9V pro
	SMC_BC_ACOK	ISL (CHGR OUT)	SMC (SMC_ACOK)	
	SMC_RESET_L	ISL /RESET CHIP	SMC	ISL to RESET CHIP to SMC
	PP3V3_S5_AVREF_SMC	RESET CHIP	SMC	U5110
	ONEWIRE	SMC	CHARGE PORT/CHARGER	
	CHARGER A/S GATE	ISL	RUSH LIMITER	On some models eg Q7180
	OLDER MAC ADD:			
	CHGR_OK	ISL	U6901	
	CGRDATA_SDA	SMC	ISL	

	REQUIRED	FROM	TO	Notes & Examples
S5 STATE	SMC_PM_G2_EN / PM_SLP_SUS_L	SMC	PMIC	U7800
S4 STATE	PM_SLP_5_L	CPU/PCH	SMC, PMIC, BUCK CONVERTERS	
S3 STATE	PM_SLP_4_L	CPU/PCH	SMC, PMIC, BUCK CONVERTERS	PP5V_S3 is the first S3 rail
S0 STATE	PM_SLP_S3_L	CPU/PCH	SMC, PMIC, BUCK CONVERTERS	Eg U0500
S0 VCORE	ALL_SYS_PWRGD	CPU/PCH	SMC	Trigger to enable CPU to turn ON

SECTION TWO: OTHER KEY VOLTAGE RAILS & SIGNAL LINES

	REQUIRED	FROM	TO	Notes & Examples
PP3V3_S5	PM_EN_P3V3S5	PMIC	3V/5V BUCK CONVERTER	U7650 Also need PM_DSW_PWRGD from SMC
PP3V3_SUS	PM_SLP_SUS_L	PCH	3V3 SUS SWITCH	U8200
PP3V3_S4	P3V3S4_EN_R	PCH	3.3V S4 Switch	U8203 PM_SLP_S5_L = P3V3S4_EN_R
PP5VS5	PM_EN_PVXS5	SMC	3V/5V BUCK CONVERTER	U7650 SMC_PM_G2_EN = PM_EN_PVXS5
PP5VS4	P5VS4_EN_RCD	PCH	3V/5V BUCK CONVERTER	U7650 PM_SLP_S5_L = P5VS4_EN_RCD
U7800 LDOS	3V3_G3H_RTC	PCH	PMIC	U7800

NOTE: VOLTAGE IN, ENABLE AND FEEDBACK ARE REQUIRED FOR THE IC TO PERFORM CORRECTLY AND RELEASE OUTPUT VOLTAGE(S) AND SEND ENABLE / PWRGOOD SIGNALS TO OTHER CHIPS.

MISSING RAILS

For any lower rail to be present ALL rails ABOVE need to be present. For example, if one S4 rail is missing you can't have any S3 rail. If you have at least one S0 rail, you know that your problem is another S0 rail and nothing else.

COMMON SCHEMATIC ACRONYMS
VOLTAGE IN: VIN, VCC, VDD, VEE, VSS
ENABLE: EN, ENTRIP
CLOCK/CRYSTAL: RTC, SCL DATA: SDA, SM

KEY SIGNAL LINES

FROM		TO	Notes & Examples
PM_BATLOW_L	SMC	PCH	Confirms MacBook sees Charger or Battery Power
SMC_PM_G2_EN	SMC	PMIC	PMIC Enable signal. U7800
SMC_RESET_L	ISL/RESET CHIP	SMC	ISL to RESET CHIP to SMC - Creates PPBUS
ALL_SYS_PWRGD	PMIC	SMC	Requires: PP1V8_S3, PP5V_S3, PP1V2_S3, PP1V05_S0, PP5V_S0, PP3V3_S0, PP1V5_S0
PM_DSW_PWRGD	SMC	PCH	PCH Enable signal. If 3V3_S5 is present, SMC must receive S5_PWRGD to release PM_DSW_PWRGD.
PM_SLP_4_L	SMC	PCH/CPU	PM_RSMRST (reset), PM_PWRBT (wake up), CLK_32K & RTCRST (clock), SUSCLICK32K. When troubleshooting verify no short anywhere, you have all PP5V_S5/S4, all PP3V3_S5/S4, no pulsing VCore or missing BATLOW.
PLT_RESET_L	PCH	CPU	Required to communicate with BIOS CHIP (SPI)
CPU_VCCST_PWRGD	PMIC	VRM - U0500	Enable Signal to create CPU Power PPVCC_S0_CPU

SECTION THREE: KEY ICs

KEY ICs	VOLTAGE IN	VOLTAGE OUT	ENABLE / REQUIRED	FEEDBACK LOOP	NOTE
ISL	· DCIN / ACIN · PP3V3 ~3V42	· PPBUS	· SYS_ONEWIRE from SMC · SMBUS from SMC · CGRDATA_SDA from SMC	· VDD/VDDP	· Triggers PPBUS .2V boost
SMC	· PP3V3 \ G3H, S0, S4 PP3V3_S5_SMC_VDDA	· PP1V2	· CHGR_ACOK from ISL · SMC_RESET_L from ISL/Reset IC · S5_PWRGD or RMC_PWRGD	· VDDA · SCL/SDA PP3V3_S5_AVREF_SMC	Main SMC power pad VBAT Required for stable S0 state
U7650 (5V/3V SUPPLY)	· PPBUS	· PP5VS5,S4 · PP3VS5	· PM_EN_PVXS5 · SLP_S4 · SMC_PM_G2_EN		
PMIC	· PPBUS_PMIC · PP5V_S4 · PP3V3_S5 · PP1V8_S0	· PP3V3_PMICLDO · PP1V25_PMICREF · PP5V_PMICLDO	· PMIC_EN3V3SW · P5VS4_PGOOD · SMC_PM_G2_EN · SMBUS_SMC_5_G3_SDA/SCL · S5_PWRGD, ETC....		Main SMC power pad VBAT * Older boards only For some models
PCH			· SMC_S5_PWRGD · PM_DSW_PWRGD from SMC · RTC_RESET_L, PCH_SRTCRST_L * PCH_INTRUDER_L * PCH_INTVRMEN*		S5_PWRGD BEFORE PM_DSW * For some models

SECTION FOUR: TESTING FOR DEAD MOSFET & IC CHECKLIST

IC	PRESENT	NOT PRESENT	FIX
MOSFET	1 Diode Mode approx .5v between source and drain in one direction but O/L in the other. 2 Ohm Mode HIGH resistance between all pads: gate, source & drain.	If these two conditions not met or MOSFET shorted to ground it is bad. Make sure gate is not open when testing.	REPLACE MOSFET Resistance test with Gate: P Mosfet: Red on Gate N Mosfet: Red on Source Mismatch will trigger gate.
ISL	· DCIN & ACIN at proper voltage · VVD pins @ 5V	· VDD missing · SMC_BC_ACOK missing	REPLACE ISL Note: SMC_BC_ACOK indicates that the DC/AC-IN voltage is ok
SMC	· SMC VIN 3.4V · RESET SIGNAL	· SMC_PM_G2_EN	REPLACE SMC Very rare to have to replace SMC
PMIC	· 3V3_G3H_RTC · S5_PWRGD	Missing LDO rails while no LDO shorted / no low LDO resistance to ground.	REPLACE PMIC U7800
CD3215	· PP3V3_G3H · Check each CD3215 4 LDOs 3.3 V, 1.1V, 1.8 V * 2 · Check no short on USB_UPC_PCH_XA/XB P/N	Missing any LDO	REPLACE CD3215 Missing LDOs but no short and good continuity with USB ROM U2890: REPLACE CD3215. The bad CD3215 is NOT boot looping and is hot.
PCH	PCH_DSWVRMEN PM_RSMRST_PCH_L PM_PWRBTN_L PCH_CLK32K_RTCX1/X2	When SMC_ONOFF_L is triggered, if no simultaneous signal (not even a pulse) on PM_SLP_S5_L, or PM_SLP_S4_L points to a bad PCH	REPLACE PCH
CPU		IF VCORE < THAN 1 OHM CPU IS DEAD	NO FIX

SECTION FIVE CD3215 FULL SEQUENCE UP TO PPBUS

	FROM	TO	Notes & Examples
PP20V_USBC__XB_VBUS	Charge port	CD3215 (VBUS)	
LDOs	CD3215	TBT ROM U2800	
GATE 1&2	CD3215	PPDCIN_GH3 5V	Later G1&G2 allow **20V** through
PP3V3_G3H PM_EN_3V3_G3H	U6903	PP3V3_G3H OUT	
PP3V3_G3H VBAT	SMC (1C2_SCL2/SDA2)	CD3215	
PP20V_USBC_XB_VBUS	CD3215 (C_CC1 & CC2)	CHARGE PORT	NOW GATE 1&2 OUTPUT 20V TO PPDCIN_G3H
AUX_DET	PPDCIN	ISL	New name for ACIN (**3.4V / 3.9V** on PRO)
AUX_OK	ISL	SMC	New name for **SMC_BC_ACOK**
Gate Q2 & Q3	ISL	Q7030~40	**PPBUS_G3H** created

BASIC POWER SEQUENCE

STEP 1: CREATE FIRST RAIL: PP3V42 OR PP3V3

- Buck converter **U6990** / **U7090** CREATES the first rail AFTER it receives the enable signal eg **PM_N_P3v3_G3H** from the **ISL**. This rail can be created whether the charger is stuck at 5V or sending the proper 20V voltage.

- **U6990** is the PP3V42_G3H power regulator IC for many MacBook models. It turns whatever source voltage into **3.42V**. It is often affected by corrosion on MacBook Airs and some MacBook Pro because it sits on the edge of the board.

- Chip number: **U6990** on older MacBook Airs & Retinas, **U7090** on 2013-2016 MacBook Airs & Retinas

STEP 2: REQUESTING PROPER VOLTAGE FROM CHARGER

- The SMC tells the charger to supply correct voltage eg 20V.

- SMC need PP3V42 and SMC_Reset_L to turn on.

- SMC will supply onewire.

- When ISL received DCIN and ACIN, it will output **AC_OK** or **CHGR_OK** to logic gate **U6901** so it can create onewire.

- If Logic gate **U6901** receives AC_OK and SMC_BC_OK it will allow **U6900** to pass onewire to the charger.

STEP 3: PPBUS (ISL CREATE PPBUS)
U7000 THE ISL9239/59 IS THE BUCK CONTROLLER FOR **PPBUS_G3H** ISL9239 ON MACBOOK PROS FROM 2016 + such as A1706 and A1708.

- Check ISL DCIN, ACIN. The ACIN voltage should be about 4 volts, much lower than DCIN due to the pull down resistors on the ACIN line.

- Check ISL VDD loop to VDDP. VDDP powers the ISL PPBUS buck converter.

- ISL will power UGATE and LGATE to open the 2 Mosfets (one chip) responsible to create PPBUS.

- ISL may short these gates if the current sensor resistors are out of whack.

- SMC communicates with ISL via SCL (clock) SDA (data) to **boost** PPBUS voltage from 12.2 to 12.6V. If PPBUS is a little low, the SMC is not turning on or these data lines are not working correctly!

IF PP3V42_G3H AND PPBUS ARE "OK" BUT COMPUTER STILL NOT TURNING ON:

- Check **PLT_RESET_L** and the other signals beside it (PM_SYSRST_L etc) on the CPU/PCH MGT chip. **CPU** needs this before it communicates with the **BIOS**.

- PLT reset missing can be caused by the clock chip (need 32 kilohertz), the SMC, PCH, bad SPI rom chip.

- Last resort, you can try to reheat the bios chip.

TROUBLESHOOTING CD3215

REQUESTING 20V FROM THE CHARGER (STEP 1) ON USB-C MACBOOKS IS A LITTLE MORE COMPLICATED

- Check PP3V3_G3H which is required to power the CD3215s. When PP3v3_G3H is shorted or absent, the device will be stuck at 5 V.

- USB-C cycling on and off is indicative of a communication issue between the CD3215s or between the CD3215s and the TBT ROM.

- Check presence of all CD3215 4 LDOs (3.3 V, 1.8 V × 2, 1.1 V). LDOs COMMUNICATE WITH THE USB ROM CHIP U2890.

- IF no short, check for connectivity with CD3215 ROM CHIP U2890.

- IF LDOs still missing replace CD3215.

- Always check if both ports read the same. One port reading 5V @ 0.12–0.25A while the other reads 0.02A is more indicative of a CD3215 issue. If both ports read 5V @ 0.00–0.02A, this is more indicative of a PPBUS_G3H issue.

- Before replacing dead CD3215s check if there is a short on USB_UPC_PCH_XA (or B)_P(or N).

- One of the most important functions of the CD3215s is to open the DC IN MOSFET to allow voltage through to the rest of the board. When PPDCIN_G3H is missing, the likely cause of the issue is one of the CD3215s is not opening the charger MOSFET.

- Usually, when a CD3215 is at fault, you will get 5V on PPDCIN_G3H on that port, but not the other. To diagnose which CD3215 is not opening the DC IN MOSFET, you will need to take 2 measurements: one to determine which CD3215 is in use and another to confirm which CD3215 is not opening the DC IN MOSFET. First, measure voltage on F3000 and F3010. One will measure 0V, and one will measure 5V. The fuse that measures 5V corresponds with the CD3215 in use.

- F3000 goes to U3100 and F3010 goes to U3200. Each fuse corresponds to a USB-C port

- If no short, and only the 1.1 V LDO is missing, it can be because the CD3215 can't load its firmware. Typically this also makes that USB port to **not** bootloop. Two options:

  o It is the master CD3215 directly connected to the SPI ROM. In that case, check continuity of SPI bus signals, possibly look at them with a scope while applying power to the board.

  o The slave CD3215 is not directly connected to the SPI ROM. In that case, it will request firmware to the other CD3215 through UART port (UPC_XX_UART_TX and UPC_XX_UART_RX). In that case, it is possible that the other CD3215 is bad.

- If other LDOs are missing but no short, replace the CD3215.

OTHER PROBLEMS

PLT_RESET_L

If both PPV3.42 AND PPBUS 15.6V are present but the fan is not spinning then there is likely a problem in the other rails being created by PPBUS. One quick thing to check is PLT_RESET_L. CPU needs this before it communicates with BIOS.

PM_SLP_S4_L MISSING?

PM_SLP_S4_L is critical: it shifts the MacBook from standby state (S5) to power-on state (S0). There are 11 or 13 conditions to be met depending on model before SLP_S4 is enabled. Five of those conditions pertain to clock signal. First off, double check PP5V_S5, PP3V3_S5, PP5V_S4 and PP3V3_S4. If their voltage is good and no short is found proceed. On MacBook Air's, you may have corrosion near U6100, U1950, and U1900. Check pulsing VCore and missing BATLOW.

SMC MISSING?

SMC is a very complex chip. It co-operates with THE CPU/PCH to manage and monitor MacBook power from start to finish including screen brightness, charging, diverse sensors and so on. At a minimum, we need to provide SMC with voltage, SMC clock and SMC_RESET_L signals.

Here's some more detail to help in the troubleshooting of SMCs.
- PP3V42_G3H provides power to the SMC chip via VBAT.
- The SMC reset chip monitors the voltage of PP3V42_G3H and if good will release SMC_RESET_L.
- The reset chip also outputs PP3V3_S5_AVREF_SMC to power SMC sensors circuits including voltage and temperature sensors.
- The SMC uses SMBUS to communicate with the ISL. The SMC monitors system input current (AMON) and battery charging current (BMON) all the time.
- The PP3V42_G3H also powers the SMC internal logic model VDDA.
- The SMC will then create PP1V2_S5_SMC_VDDC for its own sensors management module.
- Once the SMC has received power, the SMC crystal circuit will start to output 12 MHZ square clocks for the SMC.

SMC_BC_ACOK MISSING?

If the ISL is not releasing this signal, or not at the proper voltage check value of R5087 and resistance to GND on the ACOK line.
CHRG_ACIN at U7000 is about 4 V. If not, inspect the drop down resistor circuit.

U6100 BIOS PROBLEMS

If any corrosion is near U1900, replace the chip. The chip gets killed easily and will not send the clock signal needed for the PCH and CPU.
U1950 outputs PM_PCH_PWROK. Many times if this chip is corroded and PP3V42 will require a jumper wire. If any corrosion near U1950, replace it.
U6100 area. If there is corrosion around the BIOS, generally no need to worry about the bios chip; it is rarely damaged by liquid.
However, what is damaged is SPI termination resistors and traces. Verify them all.

SCREEN / BACKLIGHT ISSUES

Screen / backlight issues are beyond this guide but here are some pointers.
Verify first that SMC_LID is 3.42V before troubleshooting the backlight driver chip. If the laptop thinks it's closed, the screen won't light up.
Beyond that verifying the backlight circuit is no different than any other circuit.
Note that the screen connector is prone to shorting, when it doubt check each pin in diode mode.
If your screen suffers from the "flex gate" problem, it is possible to repair the cable without replacing the screen but it is a complicated advanced repair.

Made in the USA
Las Vegas, NV
24 September 2024

95726597R00048